I0488978

Simple Mandalas For New Artists Coloring Book

Simple Mandala Designs Beginners' Coloring Book

Simple Mandala

By : Gala Publication

2

Published By :

Gala Publication
© Copyright 2015 – Gala Publication

ISBN-13: **978-1522722243**
ISBN-10: **1522722246**

Design 1

Design 2

Design 3

Design 4

Design 5

Design 6

Design 7

Design 8

Design 9

Design 10

Design 11

Design 12

Design 13

Design 14

Design 15

Design 16

Design 17

Design 18

Design 19

Design 20

Design 21

Design 22

Design 23

Design 24

Design 25

Design 26

Design 27

Design 28

Design 29

Design 30

www.ingramcontent.com/pod-product-compliance
Lightning Source LLC
Chambersburg PA
CBHW071556170526
45166CB00004B/1703